AF506710

WILTED

HRIYANSHI GUPTA

WILTED

Copyright © Hriyanshi Gupta
All Rights Reserved.

This book has been self-published with all reasonable efforts taken to make the material error-free by the author. No part of this book shall be used, or reproduced in any manner whatsoever without written permission from the author, except in the case of brief quotations embodied in critical articles and reviews.

The Author of this book is solely responsible and liable for its content including but not limited to the views, representations, descriptions, statements, information, opinions and references ["Content"]. The Content of this book shall not constitute or be construed or deemed to reflect the opinion or expression of the Publisher or Editor. Neither the Publisher nor Editor endorse or approve the Content of this book or guarantee the reliability, accuracy or completeness of the Content published herein and do not make any representations or warranties of any kind, express or implied, including but not limited to the implied warranties of merchantability, fitness for a particular purpose. The Publisher and Editor shall not be liable whatsoever for any errors, or omissions, whether such errors or omissions result from negligence, accident, or any other cause or claims for loss or damages of any kind, including without limitation, indirect or consequential loss or damage arising out of use, inability to use, or about the reliability, accuracy or sufficiency of the information contained in this book.

Made with ❤ on the Notion Press Platform
www.notionpress.com

And in this rush,

I will try to find myself

Context

WILTED

Prologue

At fifteen, the world feels vast yet intimately personal, brimming with experiences that are often too complex to articulate. In the pages of "Wilted," This collection is a glimpse into the landscape of my heart and mind as I navigate themes of death, survival, girlhood, society, self-loathing, and love. With each day as I filled those papers with ink it never occurred to me that I would once own a book, have something to remind me that I made it. By this piece of art, I reveal a part of myself to the world that I might never consider a safe place, that I might never call 'Home'.
The poems in "Wilted" are fragments of my own encounters with these powerful forces. The musings of a young poet might not interest you, but the musing of a person who struggles to fit in and understand the daunting days of life can.
The title, "Wilted," reflects a state of immortal being— Wilted is my eternal memory, one that will never fail me. The world will be against you while you crave

success for the door opposite to the crowd; Acceptance won't be served, and Time won't cease, but this one chance of success, may open the doors to the path I have always dreamed about.
It is my hope that these words resonate with you, offering solace, understanding, or simply a mirror to your own experiences.
Thank you for joining me on this journey through the emotional and introspective realms of "Wilted." May you find within these pages both a reflection of your own struggles and a source of inspiration as you navigate your own path through the complexities of life.

— Hriyanshi

Forward

In a world often marked by its rapid pace and fleeting moments, the art of poetry serves as a sanctuary—a space where emotions can be explored, understood, and articulated with depth and authenticity. It is with great admiration and respect that I introduce you to "Wilted," a poignant collection of poems penned by the remarkably talented fifteen-year-old Hriyanshi.

Hriyanshi's poetry dives into the profound realms of grief, the trials of society, the nuances of girlhood, and the inevitable presence of death. Despite her young age, her words carry the weight of experience and insight far beyond her years.

In "Wilted," Hriyanshi captures the delicate interplay between vulnerability and strength. Her verses resonate with an authenticity that comes from personal reflection and a keen observation of the world around her. The imagery she weaves is both evocative and raw, offering a glimpse into the complex emotions that shape our lives and the quiet moments of introspection that often go unnoticed.

As you turn the pages of this book, you will embark on a journey through the emotional tapestry of a young soul who grapples with themes that many struggle to articulate. This collection is not merely a reflection of the author's inner world but also a mirror to our own, urging us to confront and embrace the full spectrum of human emotions.
It is with great pleasure that I commend you to Hriyanshi's world—a world where every word is a step towards understanding, and every verse is an invitation to feel deeply. May "Wilted" touch your heart as it has touched mine.

-A dear friend.

1

Wilted

Lost the liveliness,
Dead flowers
You might assume;
As you spell,
'WILTED'.
Disappointment leaves those lips.

But must I
Interpret it differently,
Change the perspective,
Show the beauty,
Create an art,
'WILTED'.

As I spell it,
'Forever.' I mean.
Something I can preserve,
Something that can never
Lose its beauty.

'Nothing lasts forever' they say,
But,
This wilted flower
It will.
This art,
I created, it will.

Liveliness I will bring it back,

I will show you the spark
As I spell
'WILTED'.

WILTED

13

Chapter-1

Society

WILTED

1

A Dose of Practicality

Life's good,
But the world's not;
For how to explain,
This sense,
This thought.

Hide, run away, disappear,
Don't communicate,
Or they will burn down
Your dreams.
They will make an image of you
Someone you dreaded,
of becoming
Someone your soul,
Feared confronting.

Life's good,
But the world's not;
Fear everyone around,
Be bold,

Confident,
Don't lose your mind,
But act dumb.
Or they will leave a scar on you.
One no virtue can solve,

WILTED

One no sins can reverse.

As gallons of water, you use to
wash it off.
As you become,
Scared and scarred.

Forgiveness you will beg for.
The justice you will dread for.

Explain and explain,
But the scars,
They will never wash off.

2

(Meliza Rani t. Selva, an Indian poet wrote the first
6 lines, While I continue the poem from the point
of view of the third person)

Beauty in my sins

"I swear to God,
You are the best hurricane,
I have ever chased,
Honey, I'd shatter jars
Of heart
For you."

How can you deny
Your beauty?
The blessing I didn't get to feel.

As my sins
Will they numb your presence?
Will they defy you?
For how can I make you realize
Your eyes that I die for,
Your crimson aura I crave,
And I will try and speak up,
Not stop, not until
You love the woman you are.

But society, people
As they curse you,
Make you insecure,

Until you find home
With the feeling so safe.
How shall I outweigh the burden
That they hold on to you?

3

Devil

Cherish the evil,
And destroy the good;
This naive version of myself
Whistling wind so sharp, it stings
my skin off.
But this cold hope, and
False promise,
It keeps the devil alive.
Harnesses, the beauty,
The shine and pride.

4

Can I survive? All alone…

And I will despise myself,
Every second in this unhealed
Place people call world.

As those eyes haunt 'us' down,
Or the mistaken touch,
Oh! Was that loud?

How far can we run away?
Which corner of these
Streets is unharmed.

Wear proper,
Walk straight,
Be aware,
Or decorate
        that coffin;

They sense fear be strong,
But lust
How can we outweigh that
thought?
So shall 'we' hideaway,
Or run?

Shall we be afraid,
Of our own
Shadow

For what if it's not ours?
What if it's
        Following us,
              All
                    Along?

5

Dim the sparkle

That sparkle you pass on
As your presence lights up this
room,
The room full of betrayal
We are talking about.
Those scars which once
Were deep in my thoughts,
As I see this side of yours.
Dullness and grief,
In those eyes
Which once saw terror.

That sparkle of yours don't let it
go away yet,
They will blow it off,
As they did to dull your room.
As these thoughts of yours,
They kill you slowly,
Survive my dear,
You will soon fit in the glory.

That sparkle of yours fight for it
now.
You can't let them win,
And steal your beauty.

For once and all,
Tell them your truth,

Tell them you tried and then you
couldn't.

6

On the Wrong Path?

I will hide from the world, so cruel,
I will hide my inner self, from
people so rude,
I will live the way I never wanted
to
To save myself,
To save myself from the dirt in the
world.

So, you tell me now am I,
On the wrong path?
The urge that killed,
The pain I went through,
From this world so cruel I will hide
myself.

I will run from evil,
All alone in a dungeon so deep,
Looking up at the universe,
With those bloody eyes,
I remind myself
I am a survivor.

So, you tell me am I,
On the wrong path?
Just to save myself,
From the sun so hot.

It might burn my strength; it might
burn my courage.

So, you tell me now,
Am I
On the
Wrong path?

Chapter-2

Poets' description

1

I am a poet

Use words carefully; am a poet,
I will turn them into rhymes,
Give them meaning,
Over exaggerate, make u aware,
Make you want to forget me.

Don't get near me; am a poet,
I will make you my muse
Hide you in my poetry
Scare you, blame you,
Make you regret our destiny.

Don't try to love me; am a poet,
I will detach,
As I write to breath,
Love, unknown to me
I will break your heart, hurt you
hard,
Make you feel unworthy.

Write carefully; you might be the
poet,
And if I am your muse
I will be afraid to come out of the
dark,
The worthless soul
As it resides in me,

You will enhance it more,
You will make me want to not
exist anymore.

2

The last piece of the puzzle

(I write to hide the pain, but soon the words they,
will end, they will get lost. My poems will reflect a
part of me, untold I see.... but the fire will turn
them into ashes remove my markings, unknown I
will be. And the words they will end soon, the last
piece of the puzzle, the ashes it will all go to
waste.)

This pen it can't move anymore,
This page will always be blank
somehow.
Those words can't find them,
In this lost mind of mine
"I want to write"
Is what my inner self now
screams.
But that feeling,
Where I feel
Everything and nothing at once.

Mix in with those emotions,
My perspective and yours,
My words as they come to an
end,
Imagination ceases to exist;
That one thing that keeps me
going,

WILTED

As it says goodbye Mia amour,
As the stars align,
And the waves they sink,
As I demolish,
Myself in that drawer.

3

Writers' world

You must wonder,
For why do I stop
To hear the bird's chirp.
The tap leak,
Watch
As the light turns red,
As I blank out,
"Lost minded"
In your language.
As I think deep,
Deep about the beauty,
The glory the sins,
The perfectionists,
Walking around
I enter my world.
"Writer's World".

As words, they rebel in my head,
"Poetry"
I must spell.

Memories, eternal.
Scars, unforgettable.
Love, beyond ocean.
Pain, I must smile.

Poetry,
The sense of belongingness,

Where I can hide my feelings,
Learn the depth of my thoughts,
As I enter,
"Writer's World".

4

Dear Poet

It won't be so hard to go back,
Dear poet,
Your personality,
Your identity,
It wouldn't change,
You would remain the same;
sane.

If you show them those mused
papers,
Be ready to be judged,
Be ready to have a written
description,
One you never knew could have
existed.

Hideaway and disappear,
They will take pieces of you,
Till you can't recognise yourself.
Dear poet,
Run to remain the same; sane.

5

Define your beauty

Don't get too close,
I'll turn you into poetry.
My muse,
As this paper it will reflect your
beauty, my sins.

This sweet, sweet image of yours
I will fit it in this glory.

"Oh, how pretty it is to be loved
By a poet"
It sure is,
As I will define you,
And make you learn
Your infinity.

You are wilted flowers, pretty
Mesmerizing
Cold hopeless wind, pretty
My muse
I will write about you,
I will be the writer
And you will still be words;

So before I start to scare you
away,
Before I make you immortal,
I must say

Walk away,
Betray my love, my dear.
Before you my darling,
You will become my muse.

6

Question the writer

Million feelings, no words
Ink pens, blank pages.
Vicious cycle, I am stuck in.
All that's left is to blame myself.

Rebelling noises, silence so loud.
So much to tell, abandonment
issues.
Life so long, urge to die.
And
Still
All that is left
Is to blame myself.

7

Artists

We all are artists, aren't we?
Smile to hide the pain,
Frown but not sad,
Scars underneath the cloth,
Stories untold, hidden lies
The ones that hurt the heart.
Memories, dreadful.
As we all paint,
A layer on top
Of the truth,
Of our skin,
Artists, aren't we?

8

Eyes comfort me

I see you looking at me,
With those brown comforting
eyes,
Staring into me, watching me,
Watching me as though,
You know every secret of mine.
Those eyes somehow,
As they connect to my heart.
As i stare into your,
Your warm pretty eyes,
My heart in denial,
Of being able to feel
Safe and loved.
In the world you made.

9

The View from Halfway Down

Was it for peace?
Or to end it all.
The dream that clashes with my
reality,
The drop that falls pitter-patter,
In this heaven of mine.

The view from halfway down,
As I take my last breath,
And rethink it all.

Walk closer to the ledge,
That I am standing on.

My last step,
It takes forever.
But what now,
In the air I now fly.
And the fear now it settles down.

As I breathe,
The last time now.
And with a thud,
My world it ends.

As I now drown,
In this river
Will I ever be found again?

And
With my last thought,
That takes infinity.
I
  Should
      Have
Had a view from halfway down.

10

MY MUSE

Your eyes are the ocean,
I wouldn't mind drowning in.
The soul,
I will bury myself with.
The sense, I can go numb for.

Mon amour for you,
I'd live with evil

11

Agree to disagree

They say,
"If you are loved by a writer you
never die"
But for once I want you dead.
I want you to disappear,
Not from this world
Bur from those papers in my
room.
From my notes and my thoughts.
For once I want you to not stay
But to leave,
I want you to disappear.

12

Today I learned my infinity

Falling in love with you,
Was as I fell in love with
The words you had put in,
To make sense.
As you, you are my muse,
And I am yours.

For my dreams to enter,
This world, reality.
As I saw you writing,
The never-ending chain,
As I became your muse,
I learned the infinity of me.

13

Part of me

You never really knew me.
No one did,
As this one part of me,
Never to be revealed.
As it haunted me every second.

14

In Search

In this world full of hopelessness,
I wait for you.
For how to defy this,
This thought so irresistible,
I
  Will
    Wait for you.

Chapter-3
Satan self

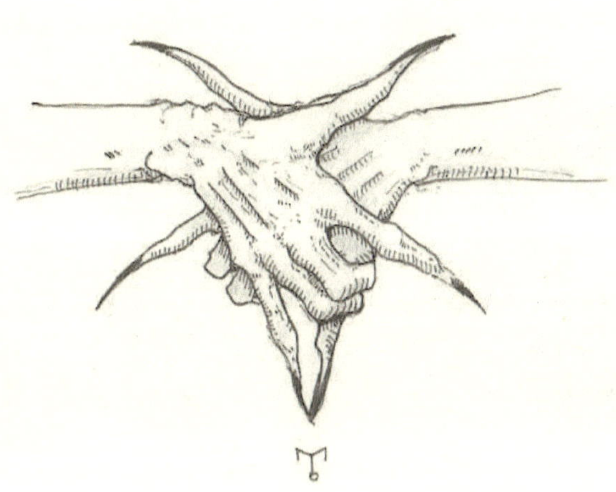

1

Description of Love

It's not exactly how it was
supposed to be.
In denial no, I won't say;

These words as they haunt me
down,
And end this world,
My world.

For as you frame that sentence,
As you describe your love,
Spare me I beg,
Incapable I must say.

Will you find my home?
Cause' I have lost mine.

In the absence of that feeling,
I crave.

Hopelessness somehow keeps
me,
Drowning in itself.

I will dig the pit and hide myself.
Somewhere you can't find me,
Because Love, I am unfit for.

2

Question to myself

Ever wondered,
Why I look in the mirror
While I cry?
Why do I let those salty tears
Defy my strength?
Make myself aware
About my miserable self?

Ever wondered,
Why do I keep clicking the pen?
Why do I let the silence?
Decide my feelings?
Let the fear set in,
And be ashamed of myself.

Ever wondered,
For why do I ask and ask
These questions
As this pen, I sit alone with?
Why do I keep on changing this
mask?

Why do I not know myself?
WHY DO I EXIST?

To make them happy?
And disappoint oneself,
To let alone my soul,

To never fit in,
Or to simply exist?

3

My dear Fantasy

Let me end my fantasy;
The one where,
I love myself.
The one where,
Everything is just perfect.

I will push myself now in the light,
Where I see myself,
The one I despise,
The one I want to escape from.

For how could one cherish
oneself?
How could this image they see,
Be unscratched, unharmed?

Now I will defy my beauty;
The one that is yet to exist,
As those eyes as they stare into
my soul.

My conscious denial,
Runway, detach "oh no",
I will hide my inner self,
The one that ceases to exist,
And end my fantasy.

4

Mirror image

Shall I repeat this again?
The story I had yet to narrate,
The blank pages that were yet to
be filled,

As I get into my head,
And look around,
The pin-drop silence,
With the voice so loud.

The remorse and the pain
Was too loud to be quiet for long,
And the betrayal,
It had changed me in many ways.

But was it the screeching sound,
that had got me thinking
Or the person residing in me?

As I try to wander,
In this other world of mine,
I saw her
I saw all of her.
Trying to find me again,
But the suffering was too loud,
And sharp.
That I had already suffocated my
ownself.

5

Adore her

I was ashamed of myself.
More than ever,
Cause' how could you adore your
beauty?
How could you love yourself?
For here I was,
All I did was pretend
Satanity of that smile to bright,
Shall I go ahead,
And not let that define oneself?

Scared of the mirror the reflection,
I grew up hating,
Ashamed of the image,
That I despise every second.

6

Comfort crowd

The drained energy,
It leaves me crawling in the bed.
The comfort place,
As I leave it behind with every
step.
As I peel off my skin,
As I reveal my inner self,
To the world full of hopelessness.

7

Join us together

Answer me, please.
As these thoughts they consume
me,
Not ready for your reply,
But too scattered to still wait.

Promises the sweetest lies,
As they hold us together,
The thread so thin,
To hold it any longer.

8

Darkness

Believe me dear it's not okay,
And the truth is yet hidden.
The sunlight that burns our sight
the dark that leaves shiver.
People that now you define,
As monsters.

9

Unworthy

I am not worth,
The tears you shed.
As I look in this mirror,
Unable to make eye contact,
As I live this life,
And as I despise myself.

I am not worthy of the love you
have for me,

I am the wrong person Mia Cara.
Save those tears,
Those promises, and smiles.

I am not worth,
The efforts you put in.
As I down in this hollowness,
Hate myself and make others
suffer.
Leave me is all that I can beg for
now.

As these beautiful eyes of yours,
They deserve more.

More than some,
'Random' person,
Which was left as a choice.

I am not worth anything,
As death is what I romanticize
now.

10

Was I So Incapable of Love

Those loud voices,
And pounding noise.
Was I so incapable of love?
That now I fear it.

As I push you away,
And join those dots,
My mechanism its cracked,
Did I do this to myself?

The blurred vision of my eyes,
As I replay those events and
those nights.
Was it all too much to ask for?
Your attention and assurance,
Was I a burden to you after all?

11

Cry for help

Afraid of living,
Fear of getting what i wanted,
And not wanting it anymore.

'Relatable' they say,
But how can I explain this?
This weird sense of tangled
thoughts.

These torn pages and,
Rebelling voices,
Death is all that I crave now.

As I scratch off those scars,
And grow as a person,
As I try to 'not rebel'

The broken mirror,
And scarred surface,
That torn page,
And tangled wire.
My voices,
They shout in a symphony,
Fix me!

And then I find myself,
In my subconscious.
As I sync with the rhythm,

As I beg myself.
Looking in the broken mirror,
'FIX ME'
I begged.

12

Secret for the world

As you disclose my secrets,
Reveal a part of me,
Masks I use,
Hide my personality.

The darkness, it becomes my
home.
As you steal that away from me,
Promises are meant to be kept to
oneself,
Not the world.

As figures I cut,
I drift away from me,
Papers I crumble,
The one that holds my identity.

Water it washes away,
The masks temporarily.

Broken glasses
Shattered mirrors
Traces the lines of my palms

Light as it bleeds my eyes,
As you disclose a part of me.

Which once was hidden
Once was a secret between you
and me.

WILTED

Chapter-4

the vicious world I made

1

Tied chains

And I will fall in love with you
All over again,
For even if I would get hurt,
Or lose myself in the process.
I would choose you.

And, I know that this dear
Plan of mine,
It has to come to an end.
But I will defy this imagination,
this dream,
I will run back to you again,

Or let me change the steps, may I
I will chain you up with my heart
forever,
So, you can hurt me over and
over,
If it takes to keep you close to me,
Mia Cara
I would give you the key to the
lock of this chain,
But you can't name the price of
your freedom,
The case the, consequence
Its costly my love
Your blood, your heart
I will have to

Detach it.
I will have
To keep you mine forever.

2

Soul voiced my head

Somehow these eyes of yours,
I am lost in now.
Addicted to that view,
View so calming, and serene,
It silences my soul.

I didn't love you by my,
Heart or my mind.
I love you with the purest
intention,
And my soul.

So as if one stops functioning,
The soul can't.
So, as I can love you,
Even when I am not mine,
Even when I'm dying.

3

Sacred?

'Satanity' or 'sacred'
What shall I name this feeling,
These sweet softening words of
yours,
'Manipulating' or 'love'.

For will you leave,
Or stay Mon Cheri,
Will this be the end?
Or something i will cherish.

Cause' the pain,
Has it been bearable,
I would have never questioned,
The 'irony'.

For did we find our
Way back to each other?
Or was this,
                a
                        coincidence,

One that should have been
prevented,
One that wasn't supposed to
occur.

4

Love exists

Love exists, of course it does,
Won't say, because of the way I
love,
Or the way I was loved.
But because of the hurt, it left.
The pain, the misery,
It put me through.
Love exists, of course, it does.
As I breathe, the awakening
sense.
As I wonder, as I dream.
As I solve this puzzle.
Mystery of love,
As it seems to make me want to
feel,
More than one should,
Love exists, sure it does.

5

Different, but just in my eyes….

Darling, you are different.
As I claim to love you,
And cherish you forever,
You my sweetheart,
You are the,
Divine soul I needed
Darling, you are different.

6

Thought about it again;

No regrets.
As two souls don't meet by
accident.

Fate, destiny,
Something might help, right?
No
    Regrets,
As I continue this cycle.

Conspiracies, I name as
Coincidence.
"No contact phrases",
As I live in this
Delusional world.

Hoping for everything to
Work out.

As I leave in the signal.,
No regrets, right?
Cause' whatever we did
Has sparkles and hope.

As these memories,
I cherished, do you as well?

Because people don't meet by
accidents,
Right?

7

Questioning your Love

Questioning your love.
What if I wasn't mine?
Lost in this space,
Or this time,
Would you search for me?
Search as you promised you
would.

For what if I lost myself?
In this process so long,
Or end up collapsing
In this world of yours?

Would you follow my path?
The one I dissolved in,
The one I perished in?

You loved me you said,
More than the sky,
More than one could love,
But will you choose me all along
Will you stick by
Even when I am not mine?

For shall I give in my all?
Or will this be some other
Experience,
One that would hurt,

One that will end someday.
Something I would want to forget,
Or something that I will take with
myself.

What if I became a burden
Someday,
What if I was not the one you
wanted,
What if this world it has,
Planned something different.
Will you wait for me?
To return back.

Will you make us want to work?
Or will this be the end?
End of something,
I would give my all to,
Something that could destroy me,
Break and shatter me.

Or will this be something
Like
"Till death do us part"?
Something
That I will cherish
And maintain till my grave?

8

My capacity

I'll always be here just in case
Is what she said.
But what about the times I missed
you?
So much that it physically hurts
my heart.

What about the betrayal,
The one they say is unforgivable,
Cause if it was forgiven.
Then the demon would be sitting
next to God,
And Satan with angels.

But oh honey,
I did forgive you.
You my safe place.
The one I crave for still,
the one I miss,
every second
of every day.
But brutal my fate,
I lost you still,
And myself in the process so
long,
Your presence, as I obsess over it
still,

WILTED

How could one hurt someone they
loved,
How could it keep their peace.

For how do I suffer more,
As I hide my eyes from yours,
How could I feel more,
Even when you took every right
from me.

9

Choice or chosen?

Why should I beg you to choose
me?
Was I not worth the respect,
Was I not worth your space?
How to forget the dismiss,
As you burned down my home.
How to forgive the hurt ,
You ask me to go through?

"Always the choice
Never the chosen"
And you proved it right,
As you make me realise my
worth.
As you make me wander in my
thoughts ,
One last time;

10

Change myself

These words the caught my eyes
"I am a leaver,
not a lover,
so, act right"

and as I chant them,
and wish to follow this mantra.
sub conscious
in denial.

how could I turn
my feelings off,
how could I give up on anyone?

I am a leave,
not a lover.
I will manifest it this time,
But one I speak,
another I forget.
Cause that's not who I am.

Or wait let's do it differently,
I am a leaver,
not a lover.
I am a leaver,
not a lover.
I am a lover,

not a leaver.
oh, there we go again.

11

Loop

I wouldn't want to do it again.
I said I promised,
But here I am in this loop,
I swore off getting tangled in.

If perfection is a mere illusion,
I begged for you to be mine.
But how could the ending of the
same book be different.,
What's the point of rereading it-
If it were to end?

They warned me,
Even the ones who didn't know
me.
And as this loop,
It has to come to an end
Yet again.

As I was tricked into sweet,
Sweet words my love.

As I find myself,.
Nowhere but this place
I got out of
I swore to myself
I did, I promise

But oh this mind, if I must start to
tell.
As I define this bleak temptation,
The one where, I know, I wouldn't
survive.
These loops that start and end at
the same time,
I have got stuck again.

12

Reciprocated feelings?

I am scared of losing you
Are you, scared of losing me?
Or am I just a rebound to you?
A player in your little cycle.

Warn me, give me signals,
I will exit, promise to not bother
you.
My existence or my absence;
does it bother you?
Or is it just me, trying to not feel
so much?

Letting go the art I never learned.
Did you learn to let go?
Let go even the ones you
promised to stick with.
So, are you scared of losing me?

13

Foolishly trust everyone

I didn't drown,.
But breathing isn't living either
As I force myself to feel.

And fake these unknown
emotions,
As I try to fit in,
In this imagination of mine.
And the idea of 'home'.

In this room full of people,
I search for you,
You the reflection of my dreams.
I forgive you I shout.
But that shadow of yours,
It fades away as if it's time.

Was I not worthy of your love?
I give you my whole,
Everyone crushed it,
Broke my trust,
Is my existing bothering
Everyone or I don't deserve you?

And now I think,
It would have been better if I
drowned.
Better if I couldn't breathe.

As all you want is,
For me disappear.

14

Stay with me

'Fate' or 'coincidence',
For was this a mistake,
That would leave me behind,
Shattered and broken,
Suffering in the pain,
That can't be endured,

Or was this our destiny
Our fate that had made us
Coincide?

The end of it,
Brutal it can predict.

Numbness, overwhelmed,
Feelings unsensed,
So you may leave now,
As the terror the thought,
All of it will kill me.

But oh Mia Cara,
Stay as though the time has
paused.
The clock has lost its power,
The world has stopped.

15

Lost my home

They say,
'Home's not a place'
And as soon as I saw you walk
out,
I realized I had lost mine.

And now as I crave your
existence,
And make those scenarios.

As I wake up, in reality
Screams they don't last long.
Not enough to make me want to
move on.

You were my 'home',
And now I have none.

'Move on' they say,
But how could I ever unlove you?
As those storming memories,
Shatter me slowly.

Hope, lost that as well
Hope to talk again,
Hope to mean something to you
still.

'Home'

Where will I find it now
Cause' even your carbon copy,
Doesn't feel that safe.

16

Blame you?

My actions, my words
Shall I blame them on you?
Victimize myself
Gain sympathy of few.

This pain in my chest,
Was it all fake to you?

Those scars on myself,
Out of control in need of help.

Shall I beg for help,
Numb myself,
Or shall I blame them on you?

You know me as you say,
So what's that mark on my hand?
And the fear of darkness?

Why do i always think twice
before
Telling someone who I am?

The urge to feel, but can't
anymore,
Shall I blame them on you?
Or it was my mind and my soul.

17

The never-so-calm heart

No matter how hard I try
I always end up by your side.
The connection
As it pulls us together.

A bond that can never be broken,
But how shall I tell you,
Something concerning.

For how I am craving separation,
Detachment, unable to breathe,
Your words, assumptions
They've hurt me so bad.

That now I am craving
Separation

.

Still, have this hope,
For the image of yours to exist,
Be alive.

Alive somewhere deep inside,
The person
That I can't let go
But now that,
I am standing here
All I want is the separation

18

Broken rules

All my nemesis,
Were your beloved.

For as they become the demon,
In our sweet, sweet bond,
As attachment issues,
It keeps us close.
But how could the irony,
Exist in real being?

All the stories will remain
unheard.
The dreams will be lost.
The promises will be broken.

We will lose our way in a tiny
black room,
'As these demons they will
become the walls.

All my nemesis,
Were your beloved.

WILTED

Chapter-5

Graveyard

1

Stimulation

As I sit in this room so dark,
I shout in the silence so loud,
Scream for help,
Help I shall seek.

Save me, but don't,
As I kill myself.
These eyes so deep, so dark,
Help me I say to myself,
With my hand around my neck.

As I lay in this dungeon so hollow,
As this page,
I fill it with ink.

The scars that define me,
The person I trembled of before,
Is someone who I have become
now.,

As I die in this blood-red bath
The numbness settled in my
heart.
Don't look into my eyes anymore,
This fear and rage,
Is all you will see.

The eyes now are shut.

And the coffin is yet to be closed,
Hands of death I have reached,
Darkness is now enclosed.

2

Home?

Emptiness,
The world full of terror,
The pain unknown,
Danger.

This wind with scribbled thoughts,
The pencil so blunt.
Torn paper apart.

The feeling so bleak,
The room so dark,
The dungeon so deep,
Drowning me,
In this world full of inhumane
people.

The blurry view,
And the clear path,
These two ways,
Separate
Me in half.

Take me to the place where I
belong ,
This room it's engulfing me,
In its darkened thoughts.

3

Question me no more

The terror the fear,
Has been stuck inside of me,
This part of me undesirable I see,
Question me no more.

This mind of mine,
Somehow lost the ability to
process these thoughts.

Somehow left me in this place,
Place so dark, so deep, so bleak.

Hide me in your shadow,
Save me,
From this demon,
This person that, I have now
become.

As I wince and wince,
As I dread for my soul,
For its freedom,

Keep me safe in this dark place.
This place called home
Is now no more to be found;

4

Help me no more

The feelings
Unsensible,
Actions unreasonable.
These eyes, so dark
So deep, not me.
These words so sharp,
Cutting right through me,
The promises so vague,
Help I shall seek.

Save me,
But don't.

Help me no more,
My mind engulfed me,
My own hand on my throat.

Shouting in peace,
In silence in pain,
This feeling so numb,
And the disapproved pain.
Now I am killing myself
In this silence so loud.

5

Kill my beauty

Was it the realization that killed
me,
Or the suffering I went through?

As I close my eyes,
And look in the image of mine,
am I still her?
Or is this my demon?

Cause' I know the pain was too
much to handle.
And I know the grief was all that I
was left with.

The realisation,
That I am no more myself.

That the mechanism it was,
Actually, my personality.

Personality of the demon,
That they made.

Now let me close my eyes again,
Take my last breath.
Shout in the silence so loud,
Let me live and survive,
These last few moments of mine,

And,
As you walk away
My dear, my lord
Let my own demon,
Kill my beauty,
My shine.

6

Realization

Realization oh it hits hard.
This world so cruel,
Unable to process,
This mind so messed up,
these tangled-up threads.

This unrecognisable silence,
The air I forgot to inhale,
Breathe;
I scream to myself.
My voice was ignored,
By my ears every time.

This blurry vision,
Haunts me every second.
Trembling soul,
Unheard conversations.

Realization of something,
Something my mind cannot
process.
Something my soul cannot bear.

7

After life

Ink I flows and it wont stop,
The pages scribbled,
Rebelling voices,
A push from the back,
Unhealthy sight.

Tears won't stop,
Images will be made,
Sore throat',
Loud voices,
Pounding noises,
And
A
Thud.

Silence, the one I was waiting for,
My eyes won't now cry,
Yours will.

My chest won't hurt now,
Yours does.

As my soul it has left the body,
Free of the pain,
No feelings,
Blank sight.

Long sleep, soulless body,
Harsh reality,
Forgotten past,
And,
All of it
Ends.

8

Ocean

The depth of reality,
As this ocean it consumes the
soul.
Insanity as it washes over the
good, deed done.
Satanity,
Rules over.
The strengthless corpse,
The darkness and the void,
As that
Ocean,
It drowns you in it.
As it echoes your sins,
The horror settled it.
The house full of darkness,
This oceans it suffocates you,
It ends the possibilities ,
It ends what's left in you.

As this comes to an end,

All I could ask myself was,

Who am I?

To keep in touch with me follow my
Instagram handle:

https://www.instagram.com/purple_.poetry?igsh=N2tyc3VqdTM4ZjNq

Acknowledgement

I would like to express my deepest gratitude to everyone who has supported me throughout this poetic journey.

To my family, whose unwavering encouragement and love have been my constant inspiration, thank you for believing in me.

To my friends, who have listened to countless drafts and provided invaluable feedback, your insights have truly enriched this collection.

A very warm thanks to my teachers and mentors for helping me in editing and improvising. I wholeheartedly thank my principal, vice principal, and coordinators for being ever-supportive and helping me in showcasing my talent.

And to the readers, your appreciation for the beauty of words gives purpose to my writing.

Thank you all for being part of this wonderful adventure.

About the poet

Hriyanshi Gupta is a 10th grader, studying at Jayshree Periwal High School poet from Jaipur. Known for her deep, thought-provoking poetry. Drawing inspiration from personal experiences and the complexities of life, she creates powerful evocative words. Wilted is her first book showcasing a remarkable young voice in contemporary poetry.

www.ingramcontent.com/pod-product-compliance
Lightning Source LLC
Chambersburg PA
CBHW021554150726
47990CB00006B/2545